THESE FIERY HEARTS

Jess Palacios

LUMINARY PUBLISHING HOUSE

For permissions, licensing, or usage inquiries, please contact: Luminary Publishing House, LLC at inquire@luminarypublishinghouse.com

ISBN (Paperback):978-1-968972-18-9

ISBN (Ebook):978-1-968972-19-6

Cover design by Nihal Zaairi (@NzgraphicsOfficial)

To the 15-year-old Jess,

Who armed herself with silence and void:

We rescued our feelings with words,
We freed ourselves,
These fiery hearts will never be numbed again.

"I have love in me the likes of which you can scarcely imagine and rage the likes of which you would not believe. If I cannot satisfy the one, I will indulge the other."

—— Film: **Mary Shelley's Frankenstein** (1994)

Table of Contents

A Note from the Author

Writing has been a part of my life for as long as I can remember, and this book is a collection of poems written from the age of fifteen to now, straight from my soul. It's my poetic journey from adolescence into adulthood, from my fiery hearts throughout life.

I'm finally ready to share my art with others in the hope of evoking healing, peace, and even love—this book, much like life itself, is all about feelings.

Playlist

Rain – Sleep Token

The Vampire Masquerade – Peter Gundry

The Summoning – Sleep Token

Alkaline – Sleep Token

The Death Of Peace Of Mind – Bad Omens

Where's My Love – Syml

Sugar – Sleep Token

Salem's Secret – Peter Gundry

Take Me Back To Eden

Shadow Talk – Magnolia Park

Atlantic – Sleep Token

Bat Country – Avenged Sevenfold

Near Dark – Yopy Mystic

Letting In – Beauville, Nombe

Blood Sport – Sleep Token

Encontros e Despedidas – Maria Rita

I Gave You All – Mumford & Sons

Maria, Maria – Elis Regina

Running With The Wolves – Aurora

Awake My Soul – Mumford & Sons

When the Day met The Night – Panic! At The Disco

Even in Arcadia – Sleep Token

Jess Palacios

Consuming Silence, Scorching Ends

Loving you is like chasing a mirage
Your touch, a ghostly camouflage
Always with me, in light and shadow
Out of reach, a distant meadow

I don't know how to stop this chase
I'm drowning in an empty embrace
While trying hard to forget
That you're not really there

The distance plays tricks in my heart
Keeping you away, from the start
With your deafening silence
My soul suffers from this violence

But I keep hunting this fire
Trying to satisfy my desire
Yet never truly seeing
That our love is always fleeting

So, with excruciating pain,
I guess I can finally admit
That our touch will never meet
Our story is short, and now, complete

Not every love is meant for light,
Some, like ours, born and die apart
Meant to mark the soul from the start
"Goodbye, I must take my heart and depart."

Jess Palacios

Onyx Swords

The persistence of life
Is such a burden nowadays
It seems time stopped for me only
And I feel lonely, every day

I try to snuff and suffocate
But grief creeps in, it's hard to escape
Like smoke through floorboards
It strikes me sharp like onyx swords

Some days grief is soft—a gentle breeze
A feathered touch to the cheek
As if saying 'I'm always here'
While consoling, wiping my tears

Other days, it invades treacherously
Gripping tight and viciously
Then it owns me wholly
Bleeding me dry, ruthlessly

This companionship, I never asked for
Hunts me down with every thought
Sometimes, I think it feels sorry for me
Yet it's incapable of setting me free

These Fiery Hearts

I'm running out of mirrors to deflect
No more masks left to protect
I guess numbness has a deadline
This void will be my flatline

Such tragic end, this has become
I thought I'd have more time to run
But feelings shackle me, make me crawl
Grief and I must meet—once and for all.

Lovers Intertwined

To be so consumed by you
That it wipes all the darkness I knew
To feel you so deeply
That it ignites my soul completely

To satisfy all your thirst
That it feeds the hunger you've nursed
To wake your dormant curiosities
And heal your hidden insecurities

To have you utterly raw and real
That suddenly, I just make you feel

Loved
Desired
Needed
Beloved

I want to be worshiped by you
And intertwined, like soulmates do
To transcend in your embrace
Each touch, a sacred space

I'm Still Broken Apart

My grandpa was a builder who guided
I remember how he cared and provided
But what I miss the most—
He made everything okay, easily almost

Fixing what was broken
Pouring love honest and unspoken
Oh how different things would be
If he was still here with me

My broken pieces, he'd fix so easily
No one warned me it would be this hard
20+ years later
I try to live for me and him
But some days the will is thin
And my best is just getting through
Why did he have to leave too soon

I don't think I'll ever live at peace
Some part of me will always need release
Shattered into a million pieces—
That's the price I pay for life that ceases

"I Desire You"

They say:

"I desire you"
but in poetry, we say:

"Every inch of my body
Was made to dance with you
I crave your touch with every breath,
Please tell me you feel this too"

Love, Transcendent

Our time here may be finite
Our love, though, feels just right
Beyond bounds of time and space
I've loved you from the first embrace

And I will continue to love you
When the sun no longer shines
When the last flower dies
And the oceans lose their tides

I'll write poems that touch your soul
Make you smile and feel whole
I'll help you dry your tears
And face your biggest fears

I'll build bridges to bring us close
Entertain you with rhymes and prose
Our love transcends time
My heart is yours through our lifetimes

Jess Palacios

To the Moon and Back, Twice...

I miss the backyard's old tree.
It's why orange means home to me.
I miss the long talks sitting by the door,
Our laughter echoing, evermore.

The jokes were funny and the honesty deep—
Halfway through, I would fall asleep.
Vovó would carry me back inside,
Tuck me in with a kiss and good night.

I miss us playing pretend with my dolls,
Creating our own games inside cabana walls.
I miss reading books by your side,
Sometimes ending in family pillow fights.

Shiny Sundays with trips to the jungle—
We'd hit the road, no seatbelts buckled
Swim, eat, laugh and play
Beautiful sunsets leading the way.

I miss Christmas Eve—even more, the next day,
Presents under my hammock in a lovely display.
My birthdays are never the same anymore.
I want to remember your voice, forevermore.

These Fiery Hearts

From the minute I arrived, you cared for me,
I was always meant for you to keep.
My heart and soul were always free—
You were my true father, you see.

I miss your voice, hugs, loud laughter,
The memories we never could make after:
Breakfast feasts and birthday celebrations—
I miss your warmth and your imagination.

I wish we'd had more time together,
I'd say this with every encounter, whenever:
"I love you to the moon and back."
But time is fickle, and ours ended fast.

I hope you can still feel my love,
Across time, space, and above.
It's strong enough to carry through,
And I'll keep living—for me and you.

Vovó (Brasil) — Translation: Grandma

And So, She Shatters

She armed herself with silence and loneliness
Her heart embraced all numbness
Becoming nothing more than just a shell
Floating away, under a self-cast spell

She knew the grip of this bitter friend
Would shatter her remnants in the end
It was a prison of her own making
Violent silence and her soul breaking

Being numb was salvation from the strain
A shield against never-ending pain
That was too much to bear
So no more feelings... instead,

She embraced all her demons
Danced with them through the seasons
The darkness became her doom
Quiet and empty: it was her tomb

Pathway

I'm done choosing my weapons
I'm laying down the daggers
I've tasted enough numbness
Almost choked on loneliness
I just want to gather roses
Leave this pit before it closes
Bathe beneath the moonlight
Wake up to the sunrise's soft light
Forget time for a while
Open a sincere smile
Barefoot in the grass
Free from my own mess

And

   Pave

      My

         Own

            Path

Walls

"Why are your walls up all the time?"
— he asks, brow furrowed.

"Because too many left me, already."
— I reply, automatically.

"So you're choosing loneliness."
— he says, quietly.

I sigh, finally meeting his eyes.
"I avoid pain... by avoiding feeling anything at all."

Roadmap to Eden

Reveal to me your secrets buried within,
The ones you hide so deeply
That ache to emerge completely

Show me what raises the hair on your neck,
What prickles deeply in your skin
I'm yearning for your good and bad within

Surrender your fears, lay them at my feet,
I'll carry them faithfully, calm and complete
Let me make your burdens obsolete

Hand me the roadmap to your personal Eden,
Your destination keeps drawing me near
I'm starving for your love, my dear

Share your truth, unaltered and vulnerable,
Show me the roots of your pain
Together we'll break every chain

Allow me to discover all your treasures,
To see you, unfiltered and whole
I want to calm your heart and ignite your soul

Arte Salva

I get lost in universes
Where I've never been before.
I live inside pages and words,
Things my soul loves to adore.
I live for art, it saved me:
Pulled me from deep precipices,
When I was ready to jump in.
Books, music, and landscapes
Seem to heal demons within,
Keeping me sane, enticed, and happy—
Arte awakens life in me.

Arte salva (Brasil) — Translation: Art saves

Surrender At Nightfall

Between these lavender twilights
My mind drifts in the distance
And it always finds its way to you
Must you haunt me with your absence?
I'm plagued by this pursuit of your presence

Wish I was brave enough to run to you
But fear sinks its claws too deep
So I lose the battle instantly
I surrender to the lack of you
It chews, swallows, and spits me full

The longer I suffer, the clearer I know
All these colors in the sky
Aren't enough to make me whole
Soon, the nightfall will be here
With its promise of silence and fear

I shouldn't be used to this, yet I am—
I'm friends with the cold and empty
They'll stay with me until the end
The silence becomes too loud
I want to scream my heart out

I'm afraid I've run out of time
And now must accept that fate
Will no longer bring me to you
With a cracked voice, I whisper:
"I knew the dream would never come true..."

Do You?

Not one single touch was ever felt
Yet full nights we still shared
Do you remember the longing we held?

Ancient promises made on the digital
Failed hopes on a screen
Missed chances and broken dreams

We created our own sunsets
Long phone calls and surrender
Do I cross your mind each 26th of December?

Gifted with a home-like feeling
From hands we never held
Being together was the best we'd ever felt

The deafening silence of my room
Swells my hunger for your touch
Did you keep my letters? The ones you loved so much?

Such a bittersweet feeling
To care about a love fated for doom
It starved and scorched us two

All the words belonged to us
It was our paradise and purgatory
Do you believe what we had was a love story?

Maybe in another life, we have a home together
Built from hugs through the night
And we dance in the dark, no distance to fight
Do you still remember?

I Had a Plant Once

watered it too much,
and it withered away.

I crave this kind of devotion—
Someone pouring themselves into me,
and choosing to stay.

Tides of You

When I look into your hazel eyes
I long to drown in their mystery
To surrender and submerge
Get consumed by their endless tapestry

My soul surrenders to the hues
Pulled into their enchanting iridescent
A spectrum of light
An ocean of colors: soft and luminescent

When your gaze dives into mine
It feels like supernovas hitting me
Shining, celestial tides
Twirling in the depths of your sea

This kaleidoscope of light
Could never drag me to shore
I was born to be kissed by it
Eternally yours to love and explore.

Offering

The
past
is
calling
A starving beast with jagged teeth
Crawls deep beneath my skin
It stalks, calling forth old debts
Awakening wounds I tried to bury
It claws its way through my mind
I'm drifting, yet still confined
I let the past devour me whole
A silent offering to the unknown
I brandish my sword, keep the beast within
Bind it down relentlessly
So it can't ever break me
from
underneath
the
skin

Jess Palacios

Beautiful Heart, I'll Wear You Now...

I want to live so intensely
To love so fiercely
That my soul feels on fire
I want to embrace every desire

I've collected too many swords
I'm ashamed of isolation's rewards
I'm ready to throw them all away
Let them rot, to their dismay

I want to collect some flowers
Absorb their healing powers
Walk free from my shame
Light up my own flame

I'll give my love with intent
My inner demons will repent
Through new paths I'll stride
Wearing my heart with pride

Home

That's how I feel about him
He's my light that will never dim
From the first hug shared
The soul recognition was declared

He turns everything brighter
Makes each heavy burden lighter
Helps me fight for what I desire
And ignites my inner fire

He is Sunday morning with rain, hot tea
He brings peace to me
A comfortable stillness, seems to say:
"I'm here now, to stay"

He heats up every part of me inside
With a simple look, no need to try
He is so much more and doesn't even realize
He's my pain and medicine, my beautiful demise

I fit in his arms like I'm made to be there
We're a perfect mold, beautiful and rare
I feel safe in his grasp, it's easy to see
We're meant for love, we're meant to be

I don't need much, just us together
Quiet nights, warm hugs, and movies
This is our version of forever
You're my home now, and wherever.

It Took Me 31 Winters to Realize

It took me 31 winters to realize—
I handed you the blade
and created excuses
for why you cut me to the bone
I realized too late, that I was all gone

Each incision carved deeper
until I was no longer myself,
drifting endlessly, near my reaper
A bleeding mess, nothing else

But the real tragedy, as I recall
with each attempt to feel nothing at all,
I was just starving to feel whole,
waiting for a savior to rescue my soul
But that never came.

Dopamine

I'm utterly attracted to the way you talk to me
Intelligence entwined with carnality
It stirs a fervor that scorches my skin
Burning desire from within

It brings me an urgency to touch, to feel
To explore every inch that you conceal
Examine each edge and curve that's real
Forget time for a while, in our fiery deal

Let's dance our own ballad without shame
No shyness, false appearances, nor blame
Free ourselves and never be the same
We're each other's undeniable claim

Let's live our fantasies without restrain
Traveling tongues that shall never refrain
Pleasure burning through our veins
Injecting dopamine straight to the brain.

I Drink From Love and Darkness

In equal measure
If I can't indulge in one, I'll pour from the other—
My soulful pleasure.

Duality

I feel my grandpa's hug around me
When I'm in nature, feeling the wind
I find comfort seated by the shore
To admire the ocean's roar

I enjoy ghost stories, scary thrills
I'm terrified of butterflies and steep hills
Crystal meditation balances me out
I love heavy metal to dance and shout

Rainfall soothes me like nothing else
I feel intensely, tend to keep it to myself
I'm a Capricorn and hate big crowds
I love admiring the moon, the clouds

I have tattoos that tell my story
From dark days to my beautiful glories
I have a soulmate, she is my best friend
I know it in my bones; she's heaven-sent

The loyalty I give is what I want to receive
I hold long grudges but easily forgive
I need time alone to preserve my sanity
Beautiful and chaotic, my sweet duality

The Truth Is...

When someone wants to
When someone misses you
When the love is true

They show up, send letters, text or call
Even if it's just to argue
Even if it's to say nothing at all

And no matter what, they will be there
For better or worse
For the glory and the curse

To make laughing a constant
Or just to be together, in silence
There's no fear or violence
Just love shared in alliance

"I Miss You"

They say:

"I miss you"
but in poetry, we say:

"I need you next to me,
To calm the tempest within
To ignite my soul on fire
And feed my deepest desire"

Lifetime Treasures

Nothing lasts forever
And yet, however
Some things can last a lifetime
Memories linger like an easy rhyme

Not the flower given but its unique scent
Warm embraces, quality time spent
Soft rain on the wedding day
Loved ones who choose to stay

Not the parties but the conversations after
Stomach tight with laughter
The comfort of a sweet childhood
That is cherished and understood

Not social posts but talking in private
Dancing the night away, loud then quiet
The scent of old family recipes
Carried through time in gentle decrees

Not expensive gifts but being together
Forehead kisses given whenever
Honest tears watching you leave
Love lingering beneath

Nothing lasts forever
And yet, however
Some things can last a lifetime
My heart keeps treasures precious as a rhyme

Shadows and Compasses

I battled to not include you in my story,
But now, if you open it and take a look...
You're on every page of my book.
You were a shadow lurking around—
At least, that's what I told myself.
I tried to keep you away, on a dusty shelf.
I denied you for so long, it ate me alive.
No more, and never again—
I'll thrive in love, no longer in pain.
Through every ache and sad moment
That I was so eager to avoid,
You were there, never destroyed.
It took me years, but I finally realized
That you are truly my undeniable,
My compass pointing north—always reliable.

A Sweet Soul, Indeed

I must've started this poem

At least six times now—

Words are falling short, somehow,

When it comes to my love for you.

School recitals and homemade food,

Rain or shine, you were in a good mood.

You cared for me—and so much more—

With a deep love from your core.

I still remember our old games,

So special, and never the same.

I've been carrying our traditions along,

And I always will, my whole life long.

I have embedded in my soul

How you love me—completely, whole.

From when I was born, to this very day,

I'm always with you, even when I'm away.

Thank you for our life together.

I'll cherish our time—always and forever.

I would never ask for another,

Thank you for being my mother.

Show Me What You're Made Of

Show me what you're made of
The wounds no one sees
Let me feel your darkness
Taste you whole—*I'll set you free*

Jess Palacios

My Sweet, Decadent Castle

My soul awakens late at night
I spend the witching hours in fright
Because you stole peace from me
And left me in this pit within

The worst part of my day
Is not the pretending that I play
But the deafening silence
That carries unyielding violence

My heart still fights this war inside:
Of thinking about us
versus
Avoiding any memory, at any cost
I'm a bloodied soldier, torn and lost.

I'm a one-warrior army
You abandoned me, not sorry
I never even stood a chance
You struck me with your lance

Maybe it's my fault, after all
For not seeing you doubt us
And I created this one-sided dream
With no walls between you and me

These Fiery Hearts

I could build my own decadent castle
With every deception you cursed me with
Maybe with time, I can throw it all back
Release and destroy every wall from within

Jess Palacios

Watch Me Ascend

I'm done drinking from this chalice
I'm longing to feel, joy or malice
So, I cast the numbing away
Let my fear face its decay

I walk among the shattered remains
Of my heart that bleed and stain
The crimson floors of my soul
How I long to make myself whole

I look at the altar I've built
Filled with sorrow, pain, and guilt
And burn it down like holy fire
Giving my soul a new desire

Ascending in courage, somehow
And unapologetically allow
Myself to embrace what I've cast away
Those long-lost feelings I betrayed

I've carved my own purgatory
Crawled, walked, punched through
Now I drink from a fountain of mercy
A fiery heart brand new

Life Happening Out There

And me, always in here
there are moments I wonder
is this love going under?

Long letters in digital
I've never had any doubt
it's always been you somehow

Somedays are excruciating
and I can't keep going
but our feelings are growing

You bring out the best
and the worst in me
the bad and good within

I keep hoping that everything
will heal if only I persist
but I'm too tired now, can't insist

Maybe our love is just a dream
never meant to be
or so it seems

No One Really Knows Me

And that is entirely my fault.
I spent years building walls—
Turned myself into a vault.

But now I long to be heard,
And that's the moment it occurred—
Perhaps that's why I'm writing:
To let my feelings start igniting.

Shrines and Silence

I used to blindly believe
You were all I'd ever need
Shrines were built that way
In hopes that, someday

I'd give you my bare heart
And we'd never drift apart
One-sided dreams, endless maybes
Slipped through my hands like daisies

Unfolded plans, unshared needs
You, the presence I never received
My treasure chest lays bare
Discarded hopes, without care

A sad truth I bear the cost
To love so purely...
and still be lost.

Hell

I've been to hell a few times.
No burning lava, no pitchforks—
Just my mind, spiraling alone,
And my heart turning to stone.

Borrowed Tales

For so long I craved
Grand gestures, loving praise,
Only to find a bitter emptiness,
Shook hands with loneliness.

I cut pieces of myself,
Turned into an empty shell,
Scribbled tall tales and stories,
Only to face a few purgatories.

Giving myself away
Was the high price I paid—
Day after day, with no end in sight,
Believing I was doing what was right.
It's been so long now,
I struggle to find, somehow,
All the scattered remains
Of my soul—free from chains.
But I feel that one day,
My downfall will be put away.
Maybe then I'll finally receive
The true love in which I believe.

Wash It Away

Life rushes by your face,
        stains your vanity with haste

        brushes against your skin,
            corrupts your certainties within

        and there's nothing you can do,
except wash your face and start anew.

Love Is Also This Tragic Tale

is it not?
to give your best,
shot after shot,
to tend their wounds
'till healing's made
only for them
to strike with a blade
gushing, bleeding,
left behind,
you wait for someone
to maybe find
your love is pain,
yet beauty endlessly
and you can abandon
just as easily.

"You"

shall always be the answer
when someone asks
what I'm thinking about

A Pirate's Life

She was done watching from the bay
Tired of waiting by the shore
She gathered her courage, sailed away
To catch the wind and seek for more.

She braved the deep, murky tide
Far beneath a storm-lit sky
With the kiss of stars so bright
The hopeful horizon met her eye.

Cast off anchors weighing her down
The winds around her were howling loud
But she didn't yield to the fear
She sailed bold, her mission sincere.

This was her treasure hunt, after all
She needed to live it through
Carve her path through drifting mist
Claim what was hers, real and true.

Realized she could swim within
No walls, no fear, no solitude to win
Calmed the waters she used to fight
Bound to meet her dawn's first light.

Jess Palacios

My Desires Are Far Too Torn...

My greed for you, is not

Arms tangled—
souls intertwined
You are the secret
I keep confined

A soft touch, almost sacred,
may be my downfall
Lips that tend to linger,
fingers made to crawl

Within all the miles of us,
a beacon's call
Can we keep dancing
beyond the nightfall?

Broken mirrors no more—
the glass lies clear, uncovered
What once was hidden now unfolds,
old bitterness gently smothered
My fears are left to rot...

My need for you, is not

I Avoided Grieving for So Long

As a way to protect myself.
I didn't even cry at your funeral—
I was so numb, a broken shell.
Eighteen years later, I can finally admit:
I miss you, with all my heart.
I'm sad, angry, and lonely—
Too soon we were torn apart.
We had so much to live together
But barely had any time.
I'm broken, pissed, and upset,
Far away from being fine.
I miss you every single day.
I need you here to calm me down,
My heart longs for your light
To take away my fears somehow.
Our time was stolen,
Life will never be the same.
"To the moon and back"—
I wonder if you still remember our game.

Jess Palacios

When Will It Be Our Turn to Fall From Grace?

In the silence between every sigh,

We bury truths we just can't deny.

Stolen moments become an infinity,

Our feelings: threshold of profanity.

Surrounded by others and confined,

We need our souls to be aligned—

Like a silent prayer to survive,

We sharpen our weapons to thrive.

Atoms born to interlace,

And a sad notion: we can't embrace—

When will it be our turn to fall from grace?

Dark eyes burning holes in my soul,

I dream of swimming in those coals.

The pain of keeping this control

Twists me inside, never whole.

Gazes flickering, always a doubt—

If just once, we could be allowed

To indulge in our deepest desire,

And burn together, our decadent fire.

Battlefield

Weapons forged out of desperation
Gripping fear and aching thoughts
Aren't they such a combination?
For so long, they're all I've sought.

One cannot dance in the dark
For a whole lifelong
Without dimming the spark
That keeps feelings burning strong

My arsenal became
More than I thought it could
Munitions, shield, and armor
A burden I've always understood

I am my own army, untouchable
I walk around the battlefield
To rejoice in my own victory
I kept all my feelings concealed

How cold and lonely have I become?
Is that regression or growth?
Deflect and avoid, I always must.
I'm loyal to my survival; it's my only oath.

A Hollowed Tomorrow

I gave you my all,

Even if it wasn't pretty or calm.

But it was all I had—

You tossed it like a fruit gone bad.

I chased your happiness for you,

As if it were mine too,

Then I realized we were together,

But I'd be alone forever.

The false promises of tomorrow,

From your heart were always hollow.

Scattered crumbs of attention,

To keep me around—your redemption.

I never asked for your love;

I just wanted to be enough

Your company here and there,

But you never really cared.

I hoped you'd love me for yourself,

But my heart was abandoned on a shelf.

I served you my heart on a silver platter,

But you threw it away and it shattered.

7 Feet

I stumble on myself sometimes,
For there are so many things inside—
Feelings, words, and emotions,
Crashing waves in restless oceans.
Some days it's hard to carry it all
Without letting myself fall.
So I taught myself to always avoid,
Staying safe inside my void.
I'm so scared most of the time,
And even lonelier, I must admit.
I live inside my head and fight,
Dying slowly, out of sight.
Wish I could break all these barriers,
But they feel like concrete—
Burying me beneath seven feet,
Darkness creeping, hungry to eat.

Sandcastle

It seems we're pouring water
Over a sandcastle.
Do you know that feeling—
When everything starts to unravel?
But I refuse to stand by
And let it all fade away.
I'm here, fighting,
Trying to make everything stay.
I'm still here,
But what about you?
Will we resist the rumbling
Or
Will it swallow us too?

Do You Think?

I feel so deeply that sometimes I freeze,
Afraid of pushing those I aim to please.
I long to be part of something greater than me
So much that it can consume me entirely.

I care so deeply for others that I forget myself.
I try to help everyone, even if it hurts my own health.
I want to be remembered, missed, and cared for—
I'm tired of being the last one looked out for.

I don't have the courage to always say what I feel.
It's a constant fear I'm afraid will never heal.
I'm terrified of not being enough,
So I've built up walls to make me look tough.

I feel extremely lonely more often than not.
I just want someone who won't leave me to rot.
I have so much care and affection to give,
Yet my heart feels empty, just craving to live.

I just want to love and to be loved in return.
Do you think this is something I'll ever learn?

I Want Someone

who enters my life by accident
but stays
on purpose...

All I Have to Give Is Love

I molded myself to fit for you,

And you'd always look the other way.

In the end, I was lonely, fading away.

You took all I had—

Still wasn't enough.

You ripped me open, tore me apart.

The saddest part? I don't regret it.

All I have to give is love—

Not a curse from below,

But a blessing from above.

Jess Palacios

I Used to Think I Had No Home

Because I never quite fit in there.
And here,
I always feel like I'm missing out—
Caught in a state of guilt and doubt.
Living abroad is a battle of choices—
The price I pay is constant,
With interest too high.
It cuts so deep, I fear it will bleed me dry.
Other moments I feel I could touch the sky.
"My family isn't here"
That's a pain I can't describe.
I'm only there once a year,
But I'm still part of the tribe.
It took me 10 years to understand:
I don't need to physically be there.
Our bond is strong, like a prayer—
Time and distance couldn't tear.

Nothing Lasts Forever. Everything Will Wither.

For too long, I allowed you
To hold the control
Over my feelings and actions—
You took over me whole.

But enough is actually enough
And I'm free from these chains.
I won't disgrace my heart anymore,
No longer bound by your reins.

You will never know
How much pain you caused me,
And that is a whole new pain,
But I finally ended my numbness within.

I'm breaking the cycle,
Letting myself live.
The air up here is clear—
I have so much love to give.

I can't forgive you just yet,
And I can't talk about it either.
The weight in my heart is lifting—
The burden will eventually wither.

Smile

I
want
to
give
you
my
love

& make you smile
I don't need anything back

just
take
care
of
it
awhile

I Guess Peace

Doesn't have to be
This extravagant thing.
Sometimes I find it beneath a tree,
With a kiss from the wind,
Among the drifting clouds,
When crows make their sounds,
And I feel this hug around my waist,
Giving me the lovely taste
Of a life not going to waste.

My Love Is Quiet but Runs Deep.

I'll love you when it's hard, even when I weep.

Won't say "I love you" every day,

But I will honor you when you're away.

I'm not loud, don't tend to show off;

I'll help when the world's weight is tough.

I won't deny my honesty,

And will shelter you with loyalty.

I'll love you on the easy days,

And even more when your skies turn gray.

Energy

My E n e r g y Is so Well Protected
There's no room for toxicity

No shallow feelings around me
I only have space for a u t h e n t i c i t y

Jess Palacios

A Kiss, a Sniff, and a Hug

I didn't live with my mãe,
So she would call every night.
"A kiss, a sniff, and a hug"
Was always said before goodbye.

When I was a kid,
I thought it was too much,
But now I know it's not—
It was simply her love
In its purest form.

She was trying her best,
Like she always did.
Just reaching out to feel close to me.

Since I was young,
Even through a phone line,
Her love would always be mine.

"A kiss, a sniff, and a hug"
Would reach me
And find a home within my heart
For eternity.

She still does it to this day,
And I do too.
It's our love language, you might say—
A way to hold each other near.

And even now though I'm grown,
"Um beijo, um cheiro e um abraço"
still feels like home.

"Um beijo, um cheiro e um abraço" (Brasil) — Translation: "A kiss, a sniff, and a hug"

Mãe (Brasil) — Translation: Mother

Ruin Me

And love my messy
parts within

I can only have you
If you can take
my chaos too

Safe Place

I really, really hope
you can have the patience
to wait for me a bit longer.
I'm cleaning wounds from long ago,
from traumas buried deep below.

I'm making of me a safe place,
filled with warmth, love, and grace.
I'm breaking the cycle—
I promised myself:
"I'll never go back to just a shell."

The Decayed Ballroom Crumbled Down

The ghosts that I knew
no longer come to haunt me.
The decayed ballroom crumbled down,
nothing but ashes beneath the sea
The endless dance
reached its final beat.
I'm awake and reborn—
the vicious cycle is complete.
No more stained glass:
the mirrors are now uncovered.
The ballroom is alive,
a newfound glory discovered.
The new pathway is scary;
the unknown haunts me,
but hope carries me along—
a desire to set me free.

Fit

when the sun
rests for the night
and
kisses the moon, quietly
I understand the beauty
of opposites
and
why we fit so well, softly.

Jess Palacios

The Ballroom of Sorrows

I dance with my ghosts in this hall
because that's all I've ever known.
In this decayed and lonely ball,
the waltz is haunting and slow.

Stained windows cast long shadows
across this empty ballroom,
and my pain softly echoes
while my loneliness blooms.

Freezing air creeps through,
the cold rattles the ancient stones.
A weary melody plays anew—
a lullaby to bury my bones.

Gilded mirrors thick in dust
reveal my ancient tragedies.
I see myself ready to rust—
the sudden death to my memories.

Chandeliers shatter on the floor,
the flames dance fast and higher:
setting fire to this ballad of horror,
inviting me to lie in the pyre.

These Fiery Hearts

Ashes in the air twirl like snow almost.
I blink, and morning stains the gloom—
I'm again dancing with my ghosts
in this endless ballroom doom.

I Feel Alot

Never too much—
Just exactly the amount
That I'm looking for.

And if you can't understand
What I'm saying,
I'm afraid my love
Isn't meant for you.

Now the Past Seems Fleeting

Like a candle melting at bay
I've endured battles bleeding
I will not be cast away

My armor is now long gone
Burned and useless, discarded
I rise anew with the dawn
My heart no longer guarded

My feelings are as strong
As the army that I've built
Now finally singing a victory song
Never again embracing cold guilt

Starving Eyes

Myself being drawn
to the most peculiar things,
had to shelter the wonders
that his personality brings.

I've built this obsidian vault
deep in my head,
where his shadows cast away
all of my dread.

I can read every smile
that he effortlessly gives away—
of sorrow, pleasure, desire,
and the one meant for my display.

I'm hauntedly positive:
his tears might be my downfall.
He is my treasured arcana,
of that I'm sure, after all.

He has these starving eyes;
they pin me to the ground.
They unravel me wholly,
our desire honest and profound.

These Fiery Hearts

His eyes, an onyx pool
simply scorching all within.
I want to get burned completely
and feel him all over my skin.

I want to bask in all his shadow,
and also in his light,
burn and surrender together
gloriously, through the night.

Your Voice, a Haunting Lullaby

Plays inside this old music box.
I'm a shattered porcelain ballerina
Trapped in a dance under your locks.

No more chords or instruments,
Our song has lost its harmony.
It's the death of the enchantment,
Just a faded, hollow melody.

Floating through stained mirrors,
I cling to my memories alone.
The lullabies you sang to me—
Now coldness chills me to the bone.

This dead end with broken chords
Is the funeral march of our story.
Unforgettable and haunting:
A macabre waltz, my purgatory.

Maybe It's Love

When someone feels
Like a Sunday
And it isn't scary

Jess Palacios

A Safe Harbor

my beautiful treasure.
Being near you
lifts the weight away,
a thousand chandeliers
lighting my way.

A light breeze,
my quiet companion.
To be held in your arms
soothes my fears,
like a sacred balm
healing my tears.

A tender touch,
my sincere smile.
To be loved by you
awakens my soul:
like a moth to flame,
I need you whole.

A soul reconnected,
my lifetime adventure.
To be your love
drives out the darkness—
like endless stars,
you fill me with light.

Sacred Whisper

One of the most vivid loves I've ever known,
He fills me with stories, truths, and jokes.
Even his silence is a comfort that heals:
My smile he doesn't borrow, but steals.

I'll never erase his memory within,
Though I've forgotten so much—so many.
The black hues he carries deep inside
Have frequencies that pull me like the tide.

His love is fierce—urgent and warm,
Intoxicating, consuming, a storm.
Deep with intent, where I ache to drown,
He's my sacred whisper; to him, I'm bound.

You Have so Much Love to Give

Even when you're hurt, you can forgive.

Only kindness pours from your soul,
Your heart's a garden: bright and whole.

I pray you never feel any doubt,
That you're worthy of love, throughout.

Your light warms those nearby,
Don't ever let it fade or die.

I traveled miles away to find you—
It wasn't random: fate always knew.

I believe our love is strong enough
To guide us home when roads are rough.

"I Want You"

They say:

"I want you"

but in poetry, we say:

"I want to be so consumed by you
that my soul burns like fire
I'd give you all that I knew
My body is yours: please nurture my desire"

Jess Palacios

The Death of All the Sorrow

This precipice I'm approaching now
Feels like a tether pulling me down
It's the death of all the sorrow—
Making me no longer hollow
I bathe in my own emotions
And become my own endless sea
No longer lost or surrounded—
But healed, loved and free

Upon My Chamber Door

Sometimes I feel it
Creeping, moving toward me,
This gnawing feeling inside
Trapped within eternally.
The darkness knocks
Upon my chamber door;
It calls out to me,
Sends shivers to my core.
But I welcome it in,
Embrace the loneliness within
As if it's my fate,
Uttermost and grim.
I hide in numbness—
It's an easy place to be;
It devours me slowly,
Yet it's a faithful friend I keep.
I know I must break
The chains of this sanctum I've built,
Not sure how long it will take
To leave this nightmare—it's my guilt.

This Is Like Quicksand

Swallowing me whole—
A sweet promise of nothing,
No feelings and no hope.
Escaping this dark fate
Is what's keeping me sane.
I'll break what broke me;
I'll embrace even the pain.
The more I fight,
The more it resists.
I struggle back, for I know it can't win.
I'll bathe in everything—
Even my sins.
In this soundless fight,
I choose my weapons right
And burst my heart open
To let it ignite.
I stand hand in hand
With a long-lost friend.
Let's go, dear heart—
We're no longer apart.

Soul Mates

I looked to your happiness
And felt it as my own.
I understood what "soulmate" meant—
Undeniable fate, full-blown.
I can feel our souls
Undoubtedly intertwined;
Two completely opposite strands,
Yet perfectly aligned.
With all its perfection and flaws,
Beauty, darkness, and light—
If everything around us is a mess,
This is the one thing always right.
We find ways to each other,
Like finding our way back home.
Doesn't matter how many lives we'll live,
Our souls will never be alone.

Jess Palacios

Backlit Paradise

You turn my crimson walls
into a backlit paradise.
My prison bars
are no longer in sight.
Let's succumb
to our deepest desire—
burn, heal, and purify;
let's ignite this fire.

Living nightmares dissipate
into a foggy haze.
Your presence—a living beacon,
casting away my empty days.

These ancient stones
never speak to me,
but your essence
always pulls me in.
Becoming a lighthouse
to my soul—
I need your light
to swallow me whole.

Wordless worship,
skin to skin,
essence, longing, and heat—
this cell no longer
holds me within.

Intertwined, endless devotion,
you're my life and death potion.
I need to drown
in your gaze,
like a moth
drawn to a fiery blaze.

Fiery Blaze

The stupor led me
Through the deepest dark.
It swallowed me whole,
Erased my spark
With the force
Of a thousand burning blades—
A soul-crushing
Unforgiving
Sinking in deeply,
Its sharp steel bites—
Cutting through me,
No end in sight.
No mercy given,
And no turning back.
Endless cold nights...
Then I hear a crack.
No surprise:
It's my bleeding heart,
And I have no more swords.
I'm all emptied out,
Nothing to ignite—
Only the echo of fear...
My ruthless fright.
Defeated,
I leave my gates defenseless.
A stoic figure,

Turning senseless,
Hoping that one day
I might come back
To turn the skies golden again,
Ending this endless black.

Jess Palacios

Burning Desire

Since day one, it felt so natural
He felt like the moonlight
With him, everything makes sense
He makes everything feel alright

What lies between us?
I won't give it a name
That would limit it tremendously
He is like my secret flame

Love lives in the details
And I live for his quiet caring
I feel it every single day
Through all the walls he's tearing

We're completely at ease
In each other's presence
There's nothing we can't share
The light and heavy of our essence

He built a safe place for us
Carved himself into me
Left a piece of his soul
With me, right here

Bursting Colors

Each time my heart beats,
I hope you know it's for you.
Longing always comes in—
I hope you feel it, pure and true.
Bursting colors when you smile—
I hope your heart beats for me too.

"I Need You"

They say:

"I need you"

but in poetry, we say:

"You calm the turmoil in my head
The balm that heals my aching dread
You vanquish any tempest in my seas
A gentle breeze that brings me peace"

Moth to Flame

Your gaze calls to mine,
Unyielding and unwavering—
Like a moth drawn to flame,
With no regret, no shame.

There's not a part of me
That can resist this twirling mess.
For us, even time will wait;
This fiery blaze will never fade.

Our bodies were meant to dance—
We will never hesitate.
For you, I'll create endless harmonies—
Perfectly misaligned symphonies.

I'd cross oceans to see you,
Embark on an infinite ride
Of joy, lust, and raw desire.
For you, I'd bare myself entirely.

Your fingers know me so well;
I'm undone by your spell.
You steal my breath and sanity away.
You're my menace—please stay

We create chaos and paradise:
No mourning, no goodbyes.
Only heat, care, and love reside—
You're my soul's destiny—I decided.

"I Love You"

They say:
"I love you"
but in poetry, we say:

"Maybe we cannot find
Paradise in this life,
But I think I see it every time
That I look into your eyes."

Darkness & Light

I have darkness inside
We've been dancing together for so long
Sometimes it terrifies me to the bone
Other times it draws me in—a siren's song

But I've finally stopped denying it
It's part of me and will always be
One cannot feel the light
Without touching the dark within

Acknowledgments

Eternal gratitude to all who have supported me on this journey.

To my grandpa, João, who left much too soon, I carry your love with me and always will. You gave me an extraordinary life, and I intend to live it for both of us.

To my grandma Iracy, mother Rossana, and aunt/godmother Alexsandra, for their unwavering love and support. You three inspire me every day to be a better woman and I hope I'm half as brave as you are.

To my husband Chris, with all his encouragement and help. You are my rock and you're always my peace in the middle of all the chaos.

To my best friend Sabrina, for being my #1 fan, supporter, and the one I'd send random poems throughout the day, half-expecting you to give up on me and my book—but you never did.

To my family (meus amores) and to my close friends (café com fofoca) who took the time to read, you know who you are, thank you for being so sweet and making me feel like a real author when I would doubt myself.

To my therapist, who helped me more than words can describe. I gave up on this book quite a few times, but you pushed me through and helped from start to finish—see? I did it!

And finally, to you, dear reader: thank you for taking these poems into your heart. Your time and attention give life to these words. This book is my soul laid out, and I appreciate you being gentle with it and giving it a chance.

About the Author

Jess Palacios was born and raised in Manaus, Amazonas, Brazil. Though she graduated with a degree in Social Services, she always felt her true calling was writing. For the last decade, she's called Southern California home, where she lives with her husband.

When she's not writing, you can find her immersed in a romantasy or paranormal/gothic romance book, traveling, drawing, or headbanging at metal concerts, not necessarily in that order. This is her debut book.